Loving The View

The Cleo And Tibbs Story

Mr. Tibbs

Loving The View: The Cleo and Tibbs Story

tellwell

Tellwell Talent

www.tellwell.ca

ISBN

978-1-77370-725-9 (Paperback)

Dedicated to:

Tibbs' Grandma
(who survived the hip operation but has since passed on).

And all his Angels and fur pals who have gone OTRB.
You may be gone but are never forgotten.

Table of Contents

CHAPTER 1

And So It Begins

I remember it like it was yesterday. 3 June 2017, the day Cleopatra came into my life for good. It was the day my world exploded, and it is indelibly etched on my heart.

I knew about the queen, because my sisfur, Patches, had conversations with her. She was an angel to my sisfur, graciously swooning over the exploits of Patches and her snake obsession. (I must admit to having the same reaction.) Cleopatra's delicate sensibilities and petrified loss of consciousness endeared her to this emotional panfur. I wanted to gallantly safeguard her despite my own disquietude over creepy reptiles. Our two hearts beat as one, and she brought out a side of me that was heretofore unheard of. We were and are the perfect match.

For those who do not know me, I will disclose a closely guarded secret: I like to flirt. Some toms have the gift of cute fluffiness (Basil, darn him, a noble Rag Doll Persian), and some have the British Blue Shorthair thing going on. (Take Lord Graydon, for example, a big city tom who is grey and white with marshmallow cheeks.) The title does not hurt things either. Both are absolutely two of the handsomest toms on Twitter and my best friends.

I, on the other hand, also enjoy dallying with the lady cats. On the third of June 2017, I commenced such behaviour with SassyCassyCat. She's a sweet, sandy-coloured Persian, and I proceeded to inform her of how charming I found her to be. Just my luck, after numerous attempts to trifle with her affections via tweets, she informed me she was engaged to another tomcat. Not that that stopped me. I continued to flatter the lovely Sassy.

This, of course, caught the attention of my Cleo. She jumped in with a tweet, reading, 'Meow such a smoothy, Mr. Tibbs.'

How could I resist? I tweeted back, 'I be a silver-tongued devil when I choose to be, Cleo, light of my life. Signed, Mr. Tibbs. *eyes twinkling impishly.*' Then I sent a photo of my hefty self in a loaf pose. I beguiled her and she, in turn, stole my heart.

As the lovely Sassy was not seriously interested in my patter, Cleo became my main focus, though I still flirted with others, such as Cleo Love (a pretty tuxedo cat with the same name as my Queen), and Holly Purr (an adorable little Maine Coon). Not to mention Basil's cat friend, the lovely

Moët (a white Persian who had gone blind due to neglect but has a wonderful home now). All these felines (and more every day, I might add) are subject to Tibbs' piffle. Have to admit, my queen is the one for me though. She has indicated that I must continue to dally with the others. How can a tom not be spellbound by such a creature?

Why she has set her sights on me, I shall never know. Make no mistake, our destinies are forever intertwined.

CHAPTER 2

Mesmerizing

The chatter between Queen Cleopatra and me began to heat up big time. She proceeded to offer compliments regarding my brawny physique. 'Loving the view,' she commented in a cheeky tweet. I puffed up proudly and fell head over paws for her inner beauty. She is a true, classic knockout. If our somewhat friendly relationship was to turn into a torrid affair, I would have to write this love story for posterity's sake.

The clincher for writing the book came when I sent out a video of my latest peccadillo. I had taken to licking my mom's ice-filled water bottle.

As the frozen water melted, the bottle began to sweat. That's where my strange preoccupation came into effect. Lapping up its perspiration is delish . . .

Her response to this was, 'One word—mesmerizing.'

Honoured by the remark, I returned, 'Right then, chapter two of our love story is written, my lady love. *This is easier than I thought.*' Obviously our passionate tale was uppermost in her mind.

Even back then I knew this would be the greatest romance ever told. More impassioned than *Pride and Prejudice* with the popularity of the Harry Potter series. And I was just the wordsmith, capable of recording this masterpiece on paper to share with the rest of cat-hood.

My Queen found her contribution to the book hilarious, claiming, 'I'm a kitty of few words, my love.'

To which I smoothly replied, 'You are, my Queen. And only one word is needed between us: LOVE. *your big bundle of imperfection.*'

I am well aware of my shortcomings; nevertheless, this does not hinder my Queen from complimenting me. (Some would class my flirting as a major flaw; not Cleo.)

We had become so close that a rather intimate exchange of tweets commenced regarding a slight poop problem she had encountered and conquered.

'So happy the royal backside is behaving itself once again,' I tweeted.

'ROTFM [rolling on the floor meowing], at "the royal backside." Mew do make me giggle, Mr. Tibbs,' she lovingly returned.

'My Queen, sharing the details of your throne/litter box adventures has me all agog. *never has poop been so fascinating,'* I replied honestly.

'Awwww, Mr. Tibbs, mew funny *giggles* mew are furry sweet for indulging my poop chatter. #TMI.'

Bringing forth her winsome giggles made my heart soar. I answered, 'No one could make royal poop more appealing. I'm just glad it's all running smoothly, if you know what I mean.'

Admittedly, the conversation was becoming a tad weird; yet, to speak so intimately was liberating. This kitty continued to capture my imagination. Such honesty and straight shooting (not referencing her poop problem here) was refreshing. The connection between us had just begun.

CHAPTER 3

Tibbs Is Smitten

A tweet full of kisses came in. (I believed it was from my friends Angel and Kobe. A sisfur and brofur who are full of mischief.) Not being sure who was inundating me with such a display, I asked, 'Who exactly is throwing their lips my way? Just wondering? *puckering up.*'

I was more than willing to play along with the innuendo, despite the fact that I did not know who wanted to shower such unadulterated affection upon me. Receiving unnamed kisses was something I was happy to entertain.

My Queen answered back, 'Pucker up, buttercup.'

Well!! The brazen hussy! 'Cleo, my Queen . . .' Impressed with her bold statement, I straightened my tie and went in for a kiss. (Don't really wear a tie, but I was painting a word picture.) I sent back more kisses. '*got carried away there.*

Signed, Mr. Tibbs, *love machine* Hee-Hee.' This was my kind of kitty. My heart began to pitter-patter.

Twitter can be so unreliable sometimes, and as soon as she saw the tweet, (which happened to be the next day) she got back to me. 'OMC. [Oh My Cat] I have just seen this, nearly missed a kiss from my sweetheart. Sending kisses back atcha.' Oh the joy. Oh the bliss. Our torrid love affair had truly taken on a life of its own.

Knowing the ways of social media, I offered, 'Not to worry Cleo, my Queen. I keep losing your tweets too. Even Twitter will never tear us asunder. *assume there's a kiss for you every day.*' She does inspire in me a romance-filled vocabulary.

'Ohhh, thank mew. Each day will be pawsome with a kiss from mew, my sweet Tibbsey.' Her adorable nature comes through loud and clear, does it not?

I answered, 'You, my Queen, make me feel like the luckiest tom on earth. Could chapter three be filled with kisses?' This electrifying section of our story was born amid a myriad of loose lips.

The fondness I felt for this plucky British Shorthair made me realize she could not keep calling me Mr. Tibbs. We had, after all, become quite close. Discussions of litter box issues and now throwing kisses, we had grown far too chummy to remain so formal.

I decided the best course of action was to dub myself with a Christian name. Something only she could call me. Can you guess what moniker I chose for myself?

Yes, that's right. I selected the name Mark Antony. It seemed fitting. The giggles that emanated from Cleopatra confirmed my grand gesture was a hit. Bringing forth such merriment caused my heart to soar with giddiness. Our destinies were truly set and I was, indeed, smitten.

CHAPTER 4
#MTIFF

Just as the relationship began to get off the ground, I had to rein things in. Not because of anything she did, or me for that matter. I had an exciting surprise for everyone on Twitter.

'May have to put our romance on hold for a while, my Queen. Exciting news. Shall I tell you about it?' I asked.

Of course she wanted to know what I had planned.

If I haven't mentioned this before, I have a career as a film critic. Reviewing videos on Twitter and shows on Periscope is my life's purpose. As such, it occurred to me to take things to the next level and host a film festival. I called it Mr. Tibbs International Film Festival.

#MTIFF.

Critiquing movies is hard work, and in order to do my best, I had to place all my focus on the job at hand. Cleo, my Queen, would have to wait. I could only hope she would understand.

#MTIFF was to last for ten days. Every time a video was submitted, I gave it an honest review. My Queen was very impressed with the whole venture. Her love and encouragement filled me with pride.

Watching over sixty videos and writing critiques for them all left me with limited time to pursue my other love. But, being a bit of a flatterer, I took it upon myself to indulge in romance and managed to communicate with my ladylove as well as trifle with the other felines who have been subjected to my bouts of sweet-talking.

The hardest part about #MTIFF was picking a winner. All the films were special, and all the hard work of the stars (and their directors) warranted my utmost attention. It was nearly impossible to choose just one. Yet, I promised them a winner which meant I had to deliver. For three days and nights, I poured over all the videos, painstakingly eliminating one flick after another until I had narrowed it down to three strong contenders.

Thinking about the inevitable winner's announcement, I had an absolutely inspired idea. I would need my pal, Basil, to help. He's a cool cat, and he agreed to broadcast the award show live on The Basil Show. (He's the star of his own show on Periscope.)

It was all arranged, and the winner was declared on 1 July 2017. Donald is a handsome grey British Shorthair who has made a number of movies which have featured on Twitter. All of them highly entertaining. He is now an award-winning leading tom. He won #MTIFF for his movie entitled "The Heist," a rollicking romp which has Donald portraying a cat burglar to perfection. It was a well-deserved win.

Basil was a riot during the award show. Normally, Bas will mug for the camera and meow up a storm. On this day, when he had the opportunity to show off his many talents, he remained tight-lipped. He was most uncooperative with his mum. (She probably did not let him play with his favourite toy!) This may have been his plan all along. Basil is a comedic genius and always highly entertaining, even when he's being ornery.

#MTIFF was a roaring success! All that was left to do was to send Donald his trophy (I had my mom do that). I was exhausted.

Once I had recovered from the festival, it occurred to me that there had not been any communication from my Queen. She had not been a part of the award show nor had there been any tweets from her over the weekend. Most unusual.

CHAPTER 5

Tibbs Is A Cad

Feeling extremely vulnerable, I was frightened in case some other smooth-talking tom had stolen Cleopatra from her Mark Antony. After discussing the scenario with SassyCassyCat, I took it upon myself to go on a quest in search of my love. Wouldn't you know it, as soon as I began to scour the earth for the love of my lives, the lovely Cleo returned to Twitter. But it was too late! I had gone off to find her, and there was no way to contact me.

I penned a letter telling of my adventure as soon as I returned, and it was the saddest tale I had ever written. Read it at your own risk, and be prepared to shed bucket-loads of tears. It is a heartbreaking saga.

Dear Cleo,

My heart aches.

I went off in search of you, my Queen Cleopatra. I believed you had forsaken me for some nefarious Julius Caesar and was prepared to fight for my ladylove. (So long as that did not involve any actual bodily harm.)

I headed for the woods and fearlessly forged a path through the underbrush. You know how wide a space that would be. Meowing 'Cleo' deep into the forest, I felt nothing would put me off finding you. Winning your hand was uppermost in my mind. Yes, I was prepared to pop the question.

With only thoughts of true love, the time flew by and before I knew it, it had grown dark. Stopping to get my bearings and rest (you know exercise is not my forte), I meowed a few more times. To my astonishment, I heard a return call. I lumbered towards the sound, believing I had found my Queen.

Stomping over tree trunks, the noises grew louder. There was a clearing, and, yes, a plump, odd-looking stray lay there chewing some grass. It was not you, my heart. But as you know, it is my mission to make every female feel special, so I, naturally, went into flirt mode.

'You look lovely this evening, my sweetheart.' I had not lost my ability to trifle with a female.

With it being cool and pitch black now, she suggested we huddle together for warmth. I, foolishly, relented.

The next morning, with a grumbling tummy, I went in search of sustenance for the both of us. I returned with an empty hand and stomach, prepared to continue my search for you, my damsel, but to my utter shock there were three tiny wriggling creatures next to her.

She told me I was a father!

Staggering backwards, I nearly ran away until I looked at those three white and ginger tykes. How could I abandon them? I took a sniff and gave them each a few licks and knew I would look after them. Great sobs escaped me when I remembered you, Cleo. I had brought shame and disgrace to our love.

After explaining all to my kitten mama, she insisted we marry right away!

The wedding took place that night, and now I am a married tomcat. We must remain no more than friends. Our love story has ended at chapter five. It shall read: Tibbs is a Cad. The End.

I spent the second night away from home sobbing uncontrollably.

Is this how most grooms spend their wedding night?

With great sadness, I journeyed home. Thoughts of food were far from my mind. That will tell you just how distraught I was over this whole affair.

So, now the story is told. Cleo, my . . . (sniffs). Cleo, you cannot ever be mine, and I shall not ever be yours. I am a broken tom.

SOB! SOB!

Mark Antony Tibbs

Needless to say, when I returned home, I was a torn tomcat. On the one hand, I was ecstatic that my Queen was safe and sound. It filled me with such joy. Yet knowing I was to break her heart left me devastated.

I could not explain to her my tale of woe face-to-face, so I decided to write about the horrendous experience. Cleopatra was distraught. An understandable reaction, of course. Who wouldn't be rattled when told the love of their lives has gone off and married another? I had acted in a scandalous manner and would pay the price. What else could I do?

Then, a beacon of light appeared. After our friends on Twitter had read about my broken-hearted blunder, they convinced me that I had been duped. Tricked into a hasty marriage by a conniving female. Oh, the guilt! Oh, the dishonour! Oh, wait a minute . . . I might get out of this.

CHAPTER 6

From Bad To Worse

Things were looking up. I was on my way to getting the marriage annulled (with the help of Lord Graydon who happened to know of a good lawyer, Bella Bassett. Yes, she is a D-O-G, but has the legal acumen of Clarence Darrow.) Turned out the female that had hoodwinked me into marriage was not a cat at all! She was a rabbit! Bella came up with a brilliant defence (temporary blindness), and I was well out of it.

The euphoria took over, and when next tweeting with my Queen, I got carried away, 'I'm truly humbled by your generous nature, babe. There's no one in the world I'd rather . . . Oh, stuff it! Will you marry me?'

I'm embarrassed to admit it, but this next bit of the story is where I come off looking like a total jerk. I was fraught with anticipation for her answer.

My Queen, of course, could not have been more gracious or levelheaded. She suggested I take some time to think over my hasty proposal.

Being the hotheaded (and in my eyes, jilted) lover, I flew off the handle. I believed the feline I had given my heart to had rejected me. Full stop. 'Obviously my bad behaviour is not forgiven. *sniffs loudly.* I'll carry a torch for you always, my Queen. But I understand. *Tibbs out.*'

I was devastated. Imagine, if you will, plucking up the courage to ask your love to marry you, and being prepared to give up all future flirting for that love, only to be told you are acting rashly. I would never relinquish my dalliances lightly.

'Too late. I'm moving on. Thanks for the laughs, babe. Signed, Mr. Tibbs. *putting on a brave front.* *hurt beyond repair,*' I shot back when she tried to explain. This was my coldhearted response, and I was stubbornly sticking to it.

'Nooooo! Tibbs . . .' My Queen pleaded with me.

Try as she might to elucidate, I was obstinate and unwilling to listen. This led to a quick campaign to replace her. (As if that were possible.) Others tried to get me to see sense. The sweet SassyCassyCat did her best to explain the misunderstanding. I refused to relent. 'You're wrong, sweetness babe, all is not forgiven and Cleo has spurned me. I'm crushed. Signed, Mr. Tibbs.' There is nothing as desperate as a brokenhearted fool. And fool I was.

I began to flirt with every lady cat I could: Holly Purr (Sweet Pea, I liked to call her); Moët, Basil's girlfriend—it was because of their relationship that she only received a smattering of my flattery (but to my shame I did ask about her sisfur, Luna); and Cleo Love (Cleo, my love, as I call this fantastically wise friend). All of them were subjected to my painful rejection. Luckily, they could see my pathetic behaviour for what it was: excruciating, disreputable conduct born of a stinging rebuff.

Then the green-eyed monster hit when Cleopatra complimented the adorable Lord Graydon. 'I hope Cleo and you will be happy together. Tibbs *wipes tears away.*' I did not mean any of it.

'LG is my BSH (British Shorthair) friend and that's all,' Cleo insisted.

I was having none of it. My ill humour continued until my pal Basil finally became fed up. He tweeted a stern, 'Enough of this! Cleo says she loves you. Be happy with that!'

'Bas, I asked her to marry me, and she told me to take a hike. My world has fallen apart. I may need professional help. Mr. Tibbs *floundering.*'

'Prove it. She did not reject you,' Basil shot back.

The harsh words stunned me. Was it true? Had I been overreacting this whole time?

I swallowed my pride and asked, 'Cleo, the others are telling me you did not rebuff my proposal, is this true? Have I been a total bounder?' To be honest, making up with her was uppermost in my mind. I did not want a future without her.

'I wanted you to take things slowly and not make any hasty decisions,' she answered truthfully.

She was thinking of me and my well-being. I felt like a heel. 'I'm a lout. A cad. Oh, Cleo, I've been acting in such a churlish manner all day. I'm ashamed. Wouldn't blame you if you chucked me for good. Signed, Mr. Tibbs.'

CHAPTER 7

The Aftermath

Once my horrendous behaviour subsided, apologizing became a way of life. It seemed like every tweet I sent to my beloved contained the words 'I'm sorry,' or phrases to that effect. 'I'm crestfallen, my Queen. If you were to say, "off with his head," I would gladly stretch my neck out. I apologize for my wicked conduct.'

I was prepared to endure endless grovelling. It felt as if I had been sent to the doghouse, which is no place for a cat.

The reason for my ongoing humble conduct was, despite my Queen's generous and lenient nature, I could not believe that she (or anyone, for that matter) could be so forgiving. What kind of angel had I gotten myself mixed up with? Do such heavenly bodies exist in this day and age? Apparently they do in Cheshire.

To say my actions were embarrassing was the understatement of the century. How could I possibly make things up to this beautiful, young British Shorthair?

I had plenty of time to ponder the situation as the chatter I had previously enjoyed on Twitter was conspicuously absent. In other words, I was receiving tumbleweeds, crickets, dare I say it, the silent treatment. Not that I blamed anyone for deserting me. The sparkling wit that was usually so evident amongst my feline friends hotfooted it, and I was left an empty shell. (Okay, not that empty as I continued to gobble up all the food.)

The only one who had not forsaken me was my love, my destiny, the greatest, sweetest kitty on this planet, my Queen Cleopatra. I may be exaggerating here, but all I had left was my catfriend. So, the decision to pour my heart, soul, and whatever talent I still possessed into making amends was an easy call. She would be my main focus.

Taking the punishment like a tom humbled this once-popular kitty. 'From now on, I promise you only fun,' I offered my Queen. I had come up with a clumsy solution to wheedle my way back into her heart. Deciding on a self-imposed exile from completing reviews of any kind, I would concentrate on my Lady Love. 'Be prepared to receive love letters from now on, my Queen,' I submitted.

'Looking forward to it,' she responded positively. There is no malevolence in this angel, whatsoever. She is pure love.

For the next week, I plied Cleopatra with verse. Everyday brought a new poem.

'Another dawn has broken.
The sun rises in the sky.
"Meow," my Queen has spoken.
Enamoured, need some pie.

Mr. Tibbs, *sending a kiss, a rose, & a heart.*'

Another of the better masterpieces was,

'Cleo,

I lost my way and you were there.
A sanctuary for my soul.
Without you, I cannot bear.
My great big heart you stole

Mr. Tibbs, *sending a kiss, a rose, & a heart*'

I must say, the lovely Cleopatra motivates a tremendous amount of heartfelt emotion from this lovesick tom. Even I have to admit to being surprised at the depth of my inner feelings.

I do believe my best work was,

'Cleo,

My heart, my soul, my destiny,
To your bosom I will cleave.
Because your love has set me free,
I've got back my joie de vivre.

Mr. Tibbs, *sending a kiss, a rose, & a heart.*'

Inundating the lovely Cleo with these poems took it out of me, and the rest of my tweets suffered. It seemed no matter how hard I tried, the ability to come up with any smooth lines for my adorable fur friends had vamoosed. I had lost my mojo. What could I do? A sweet-talking tom without words is a mum bum. I needed something to reinstate my beguiling way with words. Would my fellow felines be willing to overlook my dreadful conduct and bury the hatchet?

CHAPTER 8

Tibbs Gets His Mojo Back

After being in the doghouse for a number of days, I had totally lost my mojo. The smooth charm which normally flowed so easily was lost. The stylish quips were nowhere to be found. It became a struggle to tweet. How was I to continue to woo the ever-lovely Cleo if I could not ferret out the words to impress her?

Then, once again, SassyCassyCat broke the block. Her sweet nature inspired me greatly. A simple tweet from her offering heartfelt love had me responding, 'Sweetness, not only do I wish you the best, my hope is for your light to shine on the whole wide world. Signed, Mr. Tibbs. *feeling the love again.*

This led to a campaign of tweets that were infused with illuminating messages of passion. I sent a lovely photo of myself with my big belly front and centre to my Queen and

wrote, 'Here's another one for you, my temptress. Signed, Mr. Tibbs. *giving away wishes with a rub of the belly. What do you wish for, my love?*

Her answer thrilled me. 'To be in Canada with you.'

'Oh, my Queen, I'm going to rub my own belly for that wish to come true. Signed, Mr. Tibbs. *rolls around giggling. It tickles.*' This was exactly the sort of twaddle that I had built my reputation on. It worked and came gushing out of me like I was a love-starved Catanova.

Returning to my normal suave and sophisticated self, I offered to take my ladylove dancing. As most know, exercise is not my thing, but the ladies enjoy tripping the light fantastic, and I was more than willing to commence salsa lessons for my Queen now that the offer was on the table.

Once again, I lucked out. Cleo claimed to have 'two left paws' and was not the best dancer. I answered with, 'That's okay, all four of my paws are "left" when it comes to dancing. We shall not be competing on "Dancing with the Paws" any time soon.' Too much physical activity is for the birds, anyway.

Then, an unfortunate incident occurred. A nameless Twitterite had the ill grace to disparage my behemothness. I was not offended by the remarks, but all the lovelies I flirt with leapt to my defence.

The result: this poor person got blocked. It brought an emotional tear to my eye. My friends had truly forgiven me for my wayward behaviour.

To show my appreciation, I offered all of my feline friends (and some humans) a membership into #TibbsysAngels. If they were going to come to my rescue, I wanted them to understand just how special they were to me.

Not that I play favourites, you understand, but all of them do recognize that Cleopatra has to be my #1 Angel.

With my mojo well and truly ensconced once again, the subject of marriage kept coming to the forefront of many tweets. While this topic both thrilled and frightened me, I hoped to sidestep the matter completely.

CHAPTER 9

Avoiding The Issue

Well, wouldn't you know it, Cleopatra and I made up. My heart filled with the love that this little British Shorthair instilled in me. Nothing could make me prouder than to be in her good graces again.

My beauty Queen may have gotten a bit carried away with our reunion though. My recently passed pal, the handsome tuxedo Zackcat, asked Cleo at the time, 'Has he given you a promise ring? That happens before the engagement. Enjoy each phase of the love dance.' Zack was a true gent. I miss him every day.

Cleo answered, 'Promise ring? . . . Oh, I like the sound of that, Mr. Tibbs. *innocent ears.*' Subtlety is not one of my Queen's finer character traits.

I may not be the sharpest knife in the drawer, but I understand hints like that and recognize them almost immediately. I answered, 'As promised, my Queen. *Ring, ring . . . Ring, ring . . .* Hello, my petite.'

She obviously wanted me to give her a call on the phone that she had thoughtfully provided for me.

Then tragedy struck! My Grandma had a fall and broke her hip. The next couple days were sheer misery. On more than one occasion, the food bowl was not replenished, and I was close to starvation, as you can see.

Luckily, Grandma made it through her operation, and the bountiful supply of food returned to normal. Thank goodness. (On both counts.)

Throughout the ordeal, all my Twitter pals were kindness itself, offering up prayers and good wishes. I had to wipe away the tears. I truly have the best kitty-friends ever.

It did make me re-examine my special relationship with Queen Cleopatra. I mentioned that I had something to discuss with her. 'I know you think I make snap decisions during emotional times but through all this, I must ask an important question, Cleo, my Queen . . .'

I ran out of space and had to continue later with, 'Grandma's fall has put things in perspective. Tell me, if you think this the honourable thing . . . ? Signed, Mr. Tibbs *nervous about the proposal.* Leaving such an awkward ending was all the 140 characters Twitter allowed. Quite frankly, it set Twitter abuzz with tweets about what my intentions were.

It took a third try to finally get to the point. 'Ok, here goes. I propose . . . that we should . . . dedicate our book to my Grandma. What say you, my Queen? Signed, Mr. Tibbs. *paws crossed.*'

Being an angel, of course my Cleopatra agreed. 'Mr. Tibbs that is a wonderful idea. I love it. Kiss.'

'Hurray! I knew we'd be on the same page about this. All trepidation gone. Phew! Everything back to normal. Signed, Mr. Tibbs. *why all the wedding ring tweets?*' Have to admit, I was so focused on Cleo agreeing to my idea that I was not going to be distracted by everyone else speculating about what I was proposing.

Then my Queen sent a beautiful photo of herself in a lovely outfit.

'Cleo, look at you, all dressed up in your Scottish finery.' She was so beautiful I got carried away and told her, 'You are the prettiest kitty ever, don't forget that, my Queen, and the kindest, most loving, warm-hearted, soon-to-be-wed . . . Oops. Never mind.' I nearly made a huge blunder.

'Squeeeee, soon-to-be-wed, mew say? *excited ears,*' she answered.

I had to quickly back pedal to get myself out of this mess. I returned, 'My Queen . . . I . . Ummm . . . What I meant to say was it's soon to be Wednesday. My favourite day.' This was getting complicated. I kept losing my head and mentioning marriage. It had to stop.

I could not do it though. I slipped up again after she sent me this tweet, 'Squeeee . . . *with lots of hearts.*'

'Looks like chapter ten is being written, and I'm still working on chapter two. Slow down, my Queen. Signed, Mr. Tibbs. *may have a look in the jewellery . . .*'

'Jewellery, mew say? *innocent ears.*' The lovely Cleo dropped hints in the most adorable manner.

'My Queen, I ran out of room. I intended to say, 'I may have a look in the jewellery box where we keep the extra pens. Got to finish the book.'

'*giggles.* When you get that extra pen, have a little look-see if there's anything else in there that might catch your eye.' I had no idea what she meant by that, but it began to tax my otherwise calm demeanour.

All this wedding banter went on for a few days. Until it became too much for me. Finally, I cracked!

CHAPTER 10

Another Breakup

All the wedding scuttlebutt took its toll on me. Try as I might to avoid the subject, it continued to be a major source of tweets. My near twin and fellow black panfur, Spooky, wrote, 'You really must get on with your proposal to Cleo. I won't give up on that one.' Spooky was relentless in calling me out on my reluctance to commit to Cleopatra.

To which my Queen responded with a couple of photos of random cats in wedding clobber. She persevered and answered, 'Found some lovely outfits online that would be lovely for a special occasion, Mr. Tibbs. *innocent ears.*' Innocent ears, I ask you? Could she be any more blatant in her hints of all things matrimonial?

Spooky returned with, 'Unless he sorts his brain out, I think he may end up as a lost cause, and you may have to find a REAL tom! See what he thinks of that!' Did I claim that Spooky is a pal of mine? Hmmph, some friend!

Cleo, ever the beautiful soul, came back with, 'Mr. Tibbs is the only tom for me.' Is she not the greatest?

Another of my Angels, Toni the Tigress, a gorgeous, delicate tabby, commented, 'You love him so much, Cleo!!!'

To which the love of my life replied, 'I do, Toni. He has my heart.'

Toni added, 'He is so lucky to have found a kitty who is so lovely, sweet, and caring. I hope he realizes how lucky he is.'

My *amigas* put in their two cents' worth, 'Cleo is a lovely lady. #TibbsysAngels are glad he has somekitty like her. *hoping for a wedding invitation.*'

Toni remarked, 'Me too!!!'

That was when I had to jump into the conversation. 'Me too. Who's getting married? Signed, Mr. Tibbs. *likes a swanky celebration.*' I was up for a wedding, so long as it was not mine.

Well, didn't this set off a firestorm? Spooky, my so-called friend, put things into perspective by observing, 'Mr. Tibbs, you're dodging the issue again. It is YOU and Cleo who are supposed to be getting married! I can see you shaking with fear again.'

To say I was confused would be an understatement. I could have sworn we were talking about some other cats on the cusp of their nuptials. Apparently not. I thought it best to point out the obvious, 'Cleopatra hasn't asked me to marry her!'

Another of my Angels, Cleo Love, the wonderful tuxie, scolded, 'OMC, Mr. T. Get with the program, and ask Cleo to be your bride. You will make the most wonderpurr couple.'

Toni spoke for many when she said, 'What is he waiting for? We want a wedding!!!'

You can see the pressure I was under. Things took a turn when I found myself online searching for the perfect engagement ring. It frightened me. This tomcat felt the need to rebel. Unfortunately, it led to some serious flirting with Kiki and Fiona, two of my newer admirers. Sometimes I can get myself into such trouble.

'Mr. Tibbs, I would share my Fancy Feast with you anytime,' the lovely Kiki offered. She is a kindhearted kitty who enjoys her meals nearly as much as I do.

How could I resist? I'm not made of stone, after all. 'I'm yours, Kiki! *my Cleo, is going to be so jealous.*' I knew as soon as I sent that tweet there was going to be a hullabaloo.

Of course, Spooky jumped on it right away. 'I just can't believe what I've read, Mr. Tibbs! How can you give yourself to Kiki when you're supposed to be proposing to Cleo? Nervous?'

Well, of course I was anxious about all the tweets expecting a marriage proposal. What tom wouldn't be?

Then a tweet came in that broke my heart. Cleo sent, '*dabs tear with paw.*'

This sent my Angel, Cleo Love, on a rampage at my expense, '*paw hugs for Cleo.* Mr. Tibbs! Mew a bad kitty! *stomps paw*'

My thoughtless behaviour was, once again, losing me valued friendships. 'Et tu, Cleo, my love? *hangs head in shame.* Signed, Mr. Tibbs. *all my Angels are deserting me.*'

'Mew let food turn mew's head! Poor Cleo will never have a moment's peace! Mew must trust Cleo to give mew all mew need (although it's a lot!).' Cleo Love was pulling no punches. She tried to steer me in the right direction by adding, 'Mew is a handsome kitty cat. Cleo is very lucky to have your heart!'

Then it happened! Much to my consternation, I became aware of some photos that Cleopatra had been sending to another British Shorthair called Binky. Very alluring photos, I might add. Fear of losing her bubbled to the surface. I can get a bit jealous at times.

'She has had my heart in the past, Cleo, my love. The future is . . . uncertain, at best. For all of us. Signed, Mr. Tibbs. *being deliberately vague,* I answered.

'Mr. Tibbs, can you at least pawmise not to go running off to some vixen bunny rabbit who is trying to trick mew? I still worry about that,' Cleo Love said.

'It won't be me running off with anothcr. I wish I could say the same for my Queen. Any thoughts of brides, weddings, or diamond rings are off the table! Signed, Mr. Dumped.' I was sure she had forsaken me for another. With a broken heart, I offered, 'I may have to . . . *sob* . . . set her free. I don't deserve such an Angel. Signed, Mr. Tibbs. *weeps uncontrollably.*' I was angry and hurt! But what could I do? I was unprepared to share her with another.

My Queen sent back, 'Mr. Tibbs, I love mew!'

'Do you, indeed? Mayhap, you're too young to know what love means? Signed, Mr. Tibbs. *trying not to let the green-eyed monster prevail.' I was not happy about her sending those beautiful pictures to some other cat. The next tweet was the hardest I ever had to write, 'It may be for the best that we part. As everyone says, you deserve better. I'll remain your friend forever. (If you still want.) Signed, Mr. T.'

'Mew are my purrfect kitty, Mr. Tibbs, but, alas, if mew only want to be furriends, sweetie, furriends it is. *sad sigh.*' Cleo was resigned to the inevitable.

'I promise to be a much better friend than I have been as your tom-friend. *off to join the monks of St. Jude's, patron saint of lost causes.*' I foresaw a bleak future.

This most recent breakup had friends wondering what had happened. Cleo Love tweeted, '*scratches head with paw.*'

Then Spooky wrote, 'You sound as confused as me!!! What's Mr. Tibbs up to??'

I clarified the situation, 'The fact that Cleopatra persists in sending lovely photos of herself to every Tom, Tom, and Binky confuses me. You'd think she doesn't care.' I admit it. I was jealous despite our amicable parting.

'But . . . but . . . but . . . *wails uncontrollably.*' Cleo was clearly more upset about this split than I suspected. Setting her adrift was the only thing I could think of to do. If she wanted to pursue this Binky, I would not stand in her way.

Loving The View

CHAPTER 11

The Proposal

No communication with Cleo, my Queen, for an entire week had me a complete wreck. I shall tell you how bad it was . . . I practically went off my food! Not for long, though. While partaking in my favourite pastime—snacking—I came up with an ingenious plan where I could send her the odd (not in a strange way) tweet without her knowing who it came from. This allowed me to release some of my pent-up charm or, as some would say, blarney.

I wrote 'Everything you do is adorable.' And when she returned with giggles, I could not resist adding, 'I live for those giggles. I Love U. *kisses & hearts.*' And I signed the tweets, Anonymous. (I am very clever!) This lovely creature possessed the capability to send me into raptures, and I wanted more of those giggles. I had to decide if we were to part for all eternity or if I could swallow my pride and curb my jealousy of this Binky, and, in the process, restore the relationship with my Queen.

Thinking long and hard about the dilemma made me seek my happy place (not the food bowl this time, though plenty of popcorn was involved). I began to re-watch all the movies sent to me during #MTIFF. Videos always put me in a relaxed state. While perusing the films, I came across an amusing short entitled “Goalkeeper.” It starred none other than Binky! What?!

Suddenly, I remembered this film and my accompanying review as I had mistakenly thought Binky was a tom. *She* is, indeed, a female feline! And now I had made the same mistake a second time! This breakup with my Queen was all for nothing! Here I thought she was flirting with another tom, and all the while Binky was a girl cat! I am a nincompoop! An imbecile! A chump! So much for being clever.

Once I realized this blunder, making up was uppermost in my mind. (Mayhap, no one would notice my faux pas?) How could I possibly restore myself into the bosom of Cleopatra? Using my noggin this time nearly did me in. Then I remembered her birthday was coming up on the 5th of September. I would plan something extraordinary.

Plucking up courage, I confessed about the Anonymous tweets. As it turned out, she knew it was me all the time. Her brain power astounds me. I told my Queen I could not go on without her and hinted that the countdown was on for a pleasant bombshell that would occur the following week.

'I just realized it's my birthday next week,' she answered. The penny dropped.

'Is it? Well . . . Well . . . Well . . .' I feigned ignorance of this knowledge.

Now that I had tweeted the fact that something was up, I was a bit nervous about the timing and my ability to pull off my big surprise the day of. On the 4th of September, I wrote,

> 'You beauty! Because of the time difference, I'll be asleep when you get up, but know I'll be waiting for a tweet from you, my heart and soul.
>
> Your,
> Mark Antony.'

This was it. I had arranged for my Queen to receive a lovely gift from my heart (made especially by @clasicats) with a question attached.

My question . . . 'Cleo, will you meowy me?'

Her answer was a resounding, 'Yes!'

Now we shall spend the rest of our lives 'Loving the View.'

EPILOGUE

Valentine's Day

The 14th of February 2018 marked a milestone for me. It was exactly one year ago that I began my foray into making friends on Twitter. I must admit my mom, Minnie, and sisters, Tuffy and Patches, were far more active than I was back then.

They asked a number of toms to be their Valentine's. I inquired of a kitty (who shall remain nameless as I never heard back from her) to be my sweetheart and can only assume she was not interested in this fine hunk of tomcat. Unfathomable to me, but true. I bear her no hard feelings, though. I was young, naïve, and totally lacking in confidence. Not an attractive prospect.

Needless to say, I have come into my own over the past twelve months (not sure how long that is in "kitty time"). I am now a daring and bold—almost to the point of intrepidity—SuperTom. And all because of the love of a plucky British Shorthair named Cleopatra.

Yes, my Queen has loved me to the point where I can be myself and still reap the benefits of her tender heart.

Is it any wonder that when I saw that Valentine, the Persian cat from Noirkittymews.com, was holding a contest to write a love letter to my Valentine, I felt compelled to answer the call? I wrote,

> Cleopatra, my Queen,
>
> Meeting you on Twitter has been the greatest
> pleasure this tom has ever experienced.
> Before you came into all nine of my lives,
> I was a dumpy film critic looking for a feline
> companion to share my heart.
>
> No matter who I flirted with (and there were
> many who received my tomfoolery), I was left
> amused but lonely. No kitty took me seriously.
>
> Then, Angel Face, you turned your attention
> my way!
>
> The goodness emanating from you has
> turned me into the confident, exciting, and
> adventuresome stud muffin you see today.
> I am a better tomcat for it.
>
> The light shines from your very soul to
> illuminate my world. Each time I see a photo
> of you . . . I . . . *THUD!* (Yes, I faint at such

stunning artistry.) But it is your inner beauty which has captured my heart. The day you agreed to be my wife, filled me to the brim with joy. So much so that I nearly missed a meal.

Oh, how I long for us to be tom and wife. When that day comes, I shall hold my head high and say, "Yeah, I'm Cleo's husband-tomcat."

You are all my dreams come true. Thank you for your love.

Eternally and Gratefully Yours,

Marcus Antonius Tibbs

P.S. I promise that no asp shall ever come between us. Not even this one.'

To my utter surprise, this heartfelt missive got a special mention! I was chuffed, but, more importantly, my Cleopatra was impressed.

She tweeted, 'OMC, Mr. Tibbs, this is AMAZING. The letter is so wonderpurr. I could not love mew more. Concatulations, sweetie, mew are one in a million.'

'You inspire me, my beloved.' All credit must go to this beautiful BSH.

The thing that I adore the most about my special girl is that she has such faith in our love. She absolutely brings out the best in me and encourages my sentimental side so that what I have to offer to her, and all the world, is an infusion of heartfelt passion.

Without my Cleopatra, I would be a lonely, portly film critic who experienced love only through the silver screen. Instead, I am a vibrant, happy, lively, adventure-seeking, rather portly film critic ready to embrace all that life and love have to offer.

Tibbs' Birthday

The 4th of March is my birthday, and while I have litter mates, Tuffy and Patches, I have my own special day as I was the runt and born after midnight. Now, one would think that this, and the fact that I am a star in my own right, would lead to a huge celebration filled with presents, treats, toys, and more treats.

Not in this household!

Every year, it's the same thing, 'Tibbs do this . . . Tibbs do that . . .' If there were a tom version of Cinderella, I would fit the bill.

Luckily, 2018 was different and oh . . . sooo much better, I might add. Because of the enormous following I have (might be exaggerating there), it brought a tear to my eye to receive all the birthday wishes from my friends. All of them were kind enough to send along their love and gracious felicitations. I was truly touched.

Of course, the best part was receiving a package from my heart and soul. Yes, Cleopatra sent me something in the mail. Not only were there treats but I was given a pawsome card from my Queen. It was beautiful.

As if that was not enough to send a tom over the edge, I was serenaded by my pal Basil's mum. Having heard her sing before, I requested the "Happy Birthday" song in hopes of making fun of the human with a voice like bagpipes. But when the melodious sound of heavenly harps issued forth this time, it left me both breathless and without words.

I will NEVER allow anyone to disparage the voice of this human within my immediate vicinity again. I was besotted! I had lost my heart to a singing angel.

Luckily, my Cleopatra is the most understanding of kitties and watched the broadcast of "The Basil Show," which featured the songstress crooning her way into my heart. Cleo had to agree that it was a beautiful rendition. Of course, my Queen is not a dolt and can rest assured in the knowledge that Bas's mum is a mere human while I am all tomcat! Unrequited love is the best one can expect in this situation.

Alas, my love for my Queen is very much requited, and we have a wedding to plan!

Setting The Date

'Got a question for you, Angel Face . . .' I thought it was about time I set the date for the most important event of 2018. 'How do you feel about the month of June? And what's your favourite number?'

While my lovely fiancée was mulling over her answer, I set about arranging for the rental of a tuxedo. (Unlike Minnie, my mom, who is a tuxedo cat, if I want to appear stylish and wear the finest clothing, I have to rent it.)

Bubbles (the name I lovingly call, Moët the blind Persian) informed me that it was her mum's birthday in June. Could I use this day for the Big Event, I wondered? After all, Bubbles and her mum were having a tough time of it, what with being separated on account of her mum's courageous battle with cancer. Upon ascertaining the exact date, early in the month of June, alas, . . . it was not meant to be. Being a Canadian kitty, I had chosen 1 July as the date to announce a winner of #MTIFF which means the festival had to conclude close to that date, allowing me enough time to pick a winner.

My Queen finally answered my question with, 'Oh, I love the month of June, my handsome prince. Mum likes the number 22; she thinks it's lucky.'

Of course my Queen would pick the perfect day. I replied, 'That is a distinct possibility! You just might need to purchase an extremely fancy gown (preferably white & lacy) for the 22nd of June 2018. That's all I'll say on the matter for now. *I'm off to the tuxedo rental emporium.*' This was turning out to be flawless. We now had a confirmed date for . . .

'O . . . M . . . C . . . Who, what, where, when? Oh my, Mr. Tibbs. I am all of a dither. *purr, purr, purr.* Are you meowing what I think mew are meowing?' My cute-as-a-button BSH eagerly inquired.

'Yes, my beloved,' I answered proudly. 'I have come to the conclusion that this year, you shall be by my side throughout . . . #MTIFF 2018. What say you, my sweetheart? Shall we get all gussied up & celebrate in style?' I come up with the greatest ideas. Another film festival, and this time with Cleopatra ready to engage in the gala right along with me.

'I shall be honoured to be by your side, Mr. Tibbs. How wonderpurr. I think #MTIFF 2018 is going to be amazing,' Cleo sent back to me.

This answer left me with an odd feeling. I knew she was happy for me, but something seemed off. I reviewed our tweets, and it occurred to me that this reply lacked a certain amount of enthusiasm. 'Wait a minute . . . You didn't think I was talking about anything else, did you?' Could my original tweets have been misinterpreted?

The next day, she wrote, 'I mean, well . . . maybe . . . it's ok, Mr. Tibbs, I am a patient puss. AKA, the future Mrs. Tibbs.'

I was crushed. 'There was devilry in the air, my Queen. It is the Ides of March today, and all of us Romans tend to go a bit screwy. You're an angel with the patience of a saint. I promise . . . I shall make it up to you. Some way . . . Somehow . . .' I had disappointed my fiancée. She thought I was talking about setting a wedding date when all the while I was referring to the Mr. Tibbs International Film Festival. And when she found out, did she rant and rave like some ornery felines might have? No.

I would right this wrong I had caused. The opportunity came along quicker than I thought when she posted a lovely photo of herself.

I jumped on it and tweeted, 'And who is the prettiest feline in all of Cheshire? My fiancée, that's who!'

She, in all her modesty, sent back, 'Aw . . . *blushes.* Mew da best. *smoochies.*'

Standing proudly, and clearing my throat, I made a declaration. 'As my behaviour has been less than stellar over the last little while, I would like to formally announce to Cleo that I cannot live another life without her. Your love has set me free. Will you honour me by being my wife . . . on the 5th of September ____? What say you, my beloved? *deliberately leaving the year blank.*'

Bending on one knee, I await an answer.

CPSIA information can be obtained
at www.ICGtesting.com
Printed in the USA
LVHW051314051118
595315LV00018B/168/P